The Rights of U.S. Citizens

by Carol Domblewski

Table of Contents

How are the rights of U.S. citizens protected by law?

6

16

32

30

Citizens IN ACTION

Ezell Blair Jr. was an African American student. On February 1, 1960, Blair and three friends sat at a lunch counter in North Carolina. First, they sat at the counter where African Americans were served. They ate lunch. Then they got up. They moved to the "Whites Only" counter. Why change seats? Blair was on a mission. Today he would fight for his rights.

At his new seat, Blair asked for a cup of coffee. The waitress would not serve him. He looked the waitress straight in the eye. "You just finished serving me at a counter only two feet from here," he said. The waitress replied, "Negroes eat at the other end."

▲ In the 1960s, students protested unequal treatment by sitting for hours or even days at lunch counters that refused to serve African Americans.

Then Blair and his friends made history. They held the first sit-in. A sit-in is a type of protest. Blair and his friends planned to sit until they were served. They were putting their rights into action. They sat at the counter all day. They were never served.

Blair and his friends were against segregation (seh-grih-GAY-shun). Segregation is the separation of black and white people. Blair thought this law was unfair.

Should asking for a cup of coffee be against the law?

The Declaration of Independence says, "All men are created equal." Blair and his friends wanted to claim their equal rights.

Personal Perspectives

In a sense we've come . . . to cash a check. When the architects of our republic [the founding fathers] wrote the magnificent words of the Constitution and the Declaration of Independence, they were signing a . . . promise that all men, yes, black men as well as white men, would be guaranteed the unalienable rights of life, liberty, and the pursuit of happiness.

—Martin Luther King Jr. in his speech "I Have a Dream," 1963

Being a U.S. Citizen

What is a U.S. citizen?

The United States is a **democracy** (dih-MAH-kruh-see). In this government, **citizens** (SIH-tih-zenz) choose their leaders. In the United States, citizens have many special rights.

In the United States, people have the right to "life, liberty, and the pursuit of happiness." These are powerful words. What do these words mean? These words mean that people have the right to live freely. They have the right to make their dreams come true. Long ago, colonists (KAH-luh-nists) fought to win these rights. The students at the lunch counter were also fighting for these rights.

The ROOT of the MEANING

The word citizen comes from the old French *citeain* and the English *denizen*. It means "inhabitant of a country."

In a democracy, citizens vote in regularly held elections. ▶

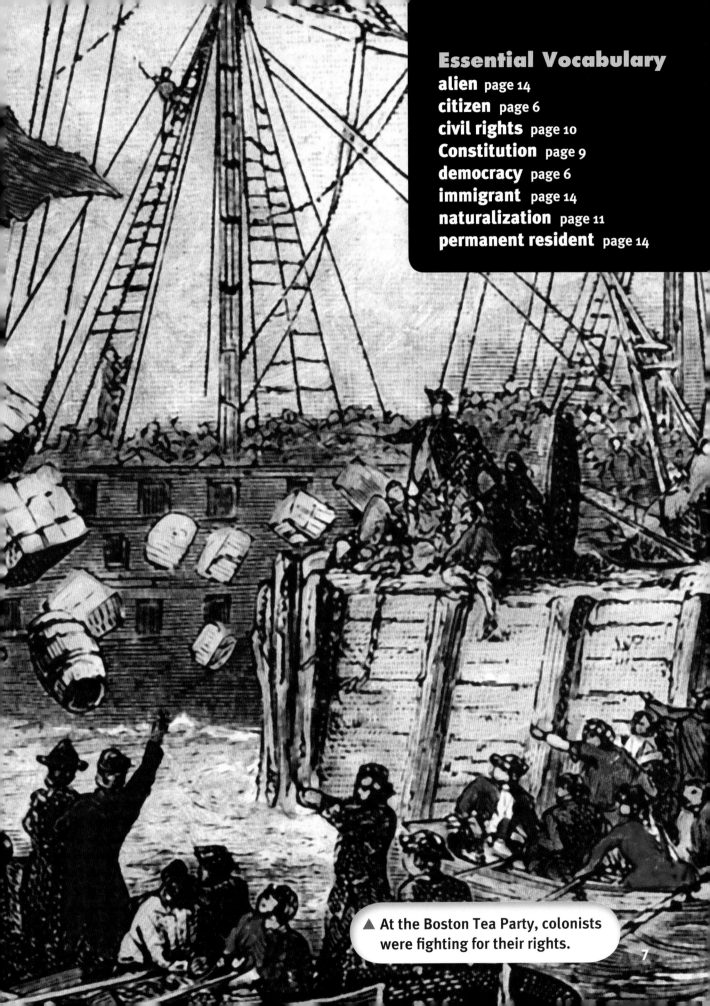

▲ At the Boston Tea Party, colonists were fighting for their rights.

Principles of Our Democracy

A democracy is a type of government. Citizens make the laws and run the government. That is how the government works in the United States. Citizens are guaranteed certain rights. These rights come from these basic principles, or ideas:

Power of the people.

In a democracy, citizens make decisions. They vote for their leaders.

Free and fair elections.

Leaders are elected fairly. No one pays to vote. No one has to pass a test to vote. Voting is done by secret ballot. This means people can vote in private for who they want.

Equal protection under the law.

All citizens must follow the same set of laws. No one is above the law. The rich, poor, weak, and strong are equal under the law.

Basic human rights.

You have the right to life, to liberty, and to pursuing happiness. You can worship as you wish. You can say what you think. You have the right to an education. You also have the right to earn a living.

Majority rule, minority rights.

The majority, or the larger group, makes the laws. But the rights of the minority, or smaller groups, are protected. The laws must be fair to everyone.

> A democracy is a form of government in which the citizens make the laws and run the government.

MR.PRESIDENT HOW LONG MUST WOMEN WAIT FOR LIBERTY

The same values over time.
As times change, the laws can change, too. Even the **Constitution** (kahn-stih-TOO-shun) can change. The country values discussion and compromise. The country values tolerance. Tolerance is the willingness to respect or accept the customs, beliefs, or opinions of others.

Civilian authority.
Elected leaders control the military, or armed forces. This means that citizens have power even during war.

These principles make sure that all citizens have the right to vote and the right to free speech.

Checkpoint

Think About It

The word democracy comes from the Greek word *demos*, which means "people." In our democracy, what powers do the people hold?

Historical Perspectives
Our Imperfect Democracy

Democracy is not a synonym for *perfect*. In a democracy, citizens make the laws. The citizens are not perfect. They are human. Democracies can change. The people are free to speak out and fight for their rights. Through peaceful protest, many groups of citizens have worked to change America for the better.

▲ In the 1960s, people fought and won civil rights for African Americans.

◄ Throughout American history, groups have used picketing as a peaceful way of changing things. Here in Washington, D.C., women picket for the right to vote. In 1920, women won the right to vote in national elections.

Seeking Democracy

The U.S. gives many rights to its citizens. People in most other places in the world do not have these rights. Some people come to the U.S. for those rights.

Religious freedom is an important right. About 100 years ago, Jewish people in Russia did not have rights. They were attacked for their beliefs. Many Russian Jews were killed. Their homes were destroyed. As a result, two million fled. These Jewish people left Russia. They left to find the freedom to worship, or pray, as they wished. Most came to the United States. They were looking for **civil rights** (SIH-vul RITES). In the United States, they could vote. They could speak freely. Most importantly, they could worship without facing harm.

▲ Cubans were not allowed to leave Cuba legally, so people desperate for freedom made the ninety-mile trip to Florida in homemade boats like this one. The trip was dangerous, and some lost their lives.

The U.S. accepts people who do not have civil rights in their own countries. In 1959, Fidel Castro became the leader of Cuba. Anyone who spoke out against his government was in danger.

From 1959 to the present, many Cubans have left Cuba. They left to find freedom in the United States. Hundreds of thousands of Cubans have come to the United States. They have come for freedom of speech and other rights.

▲ Russian immigrants came to the United States for freedom.

Text Structure: Cause and Effect

The words *as a result* tell us the author is using cause-and-effect text structure.

Becoming a Citizen

Most people who move to the United States want to be citizens. They want to enjoy the rights of full citizenship. You can become a U.S. citizen in two ways. The first way is by birth. The second way is by law. A person who is born in the U.S. is a citizen. A person born outside the U.S. to parents who are U.S. citizens is a citizen, too.

A person who wants to become a citizen must go through a long process. The process is called **naturalization** (na-chuh-ruh-lih-ZAY-shun).

Naturalization takes about five years. First, a person must complete an application. Then the person is fingerprinted and provides photographs. Next, the person has an interview and takes a test. The test shows that the

There are only two ways to become a U.S. citizen: either by birth or by law.

person understands English. The test also shows that the person knows the laws. After they pass, they go to a naturalization ceremony. Finally, the person is sworn in as a U.S. citizen.

▼ **These people have completed the citizenship process.**

11

Primary Sources

The United States
Citizenship Test

People looking to become citizens go through an interview process. Part of the interview process involves answering questions about the United States. People answer the questions as part of the interview. Here are some sample questions that people becoming citizens answer.

Between 1892 and 1954, over 12 million people from other countries entered the U.S. through Ellis Island, a small island in New York Harbor. ▶

1. What is the Constitution?

2. What is the Bill of Rights?

3. What were the 13 original colonies?

4. Whose rights are guaranteed by the Constitution and the Bill of Rights?

5. Name the rights guaranteed by the First Amendment.

6. What do the stripes on the flag mean?

7. What are the three branches of our government?

8. How many senators are there in Congress?

9. What is the basic belief of the Declaration of Independence?

10. Who was president during the Civil War?

11. Who helped the Pilgrims in America?

12. What is the introduction to the Constitution called?

13. What three requirements must a presidential candidate meet?

Answers:

1. The supreme law of the land
2. The first ten amendments of the Constitution
3. Colonies: NY, NJ, PA, MA, NH, DE, VA, NC, SC, MD, CT, RI, GA
4. Everyone (citizens and noncitizens) living in the United States
5. Freedom of speech, press, religion, peaceable assembly, and requesting change of the government
6. The 13 red and white stripes represent the first 13 colonies.
7. Legislative (Congress = Senate + House of Representatives), Executive (President + Cabinet), Judicial (Supreme Court)
8. 100
9. That all men (and women) are created equal
10. Abraham Lincoln
11. Native Americans
12. The Preamble
13. 1. Natural-born citizen; 2. At least 35 years of age; 3. Live in the U.S. at least 14 years prior to election

Aliens and Permanent Residents

Some people who live in the United States are called **aliens** (AY-lee-enz). Aliens are people who were not born here. Aliens have many of the same rights as citizens. But they cannot vote.

Some aliens are called **permanent residents** (PER-muh-nent REH-zih-dents). These people plan to stay in the country. They have entered the country by legal means. They may or may not choose to become citizens.

Many **immigrants** (IH-mih-grunts) have come to the United States over the years. Immigrants are people who come to live in a country in which they were not born. For years, these people have helped our nation grow and prosper.

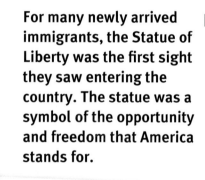

For many newly arrived immigrants, the Statue of Liberty was the first sight they saw entering the country. The statue was a symbol of the opportunity and freedom that America stands for.

SUMMING UP

- The U.S. is a democracy run by its citizens. Power rests with the people and we live by the rule of law.

- All people born in the U.S. are citizens and are granted the most basic rights of life, liberty, and the pursuit of happiness.

- Many people in countries around the world do not have these basic rights. Some of these people want to become U.S. citizens to gain those rights.

- People who wish to become U.S. citizens must go through a long process to become naturalized citizens.

Putting It All Together

Choose one of the activities below. Work independently, in pairs, or in groups. Share your answer and what you have learned with the class.

1. Reread the Principles of Our Democracy on pages 8–9. Choose one principle. Draw one example of how that principle works today.

2. A person from another country asks you to tell him or her why it is great to be a U.S. citizen. How would you respond? Act out the scene with a partner.

3. Research U.S. immigration over the last two hundred years. Create a time line that tells the story of how, when, and why certain groups came to America.

Fighting for
Citizens' Rights

What are the rights of U.S. citizens, as defined by the Constitution and the Bill of Rights?

Primary Sources

This historic painting by John Trumbull shows the signing of the Declaration of Independence in Philadelphia on July 4, 1776. Thomas Jefferson, standing in the reddish-brown vest, is presenting the document to John Hancock, the president of the Congress. Hancock was the first to sign the Declaration. Benjamin Franklin is standing to the right of Jefferson. John Adams is at the far left of the standing men. Look closely and you'll see that Jefferson is standing on Adams's foot. Trumbull sketched the men and the room from life.

n the 1700s, Great Britain ruled the thirteen American colonies. The colonists did not like British rule. They did not think the British king was fair. They wanted to be free. The Declaration of Independence was signed on July 4, 1776. This document declared America independent, or free.

The colonists who signed the document wanted to start a free nation. They wanted a government run by its citizens. The first section of the Declaration talks about citizens' rights.

This paragraph has some great ideas. "All men are created equal" means that every citizen has equal rights. This paragraph also says that the government gets its power from the people. Giving citizens so much power was a new idea.

Primary Sources

"We hold these truths to be self-evident, that all men are created equal, that they are endowed by their creator with certain unalienable rights, that among these are life, liberty and the pursuit of happiness. That to secure these rights, governments are instituted among men, deriving their just powers from the consent of the governed."

—The Declaration of Independence

The Constitution

The document alone did not free the colonists. They would also have to fight the British. American and British soldiers fought for several years. At last the Americans defeated the British in 1781. The colonists were now free to form a new nation. It would be a nation ruled by laws, not kings.

American leaders had to plan a government. The nation's government would be based on citizens' rights. But the government also had to be strong enough to get things done.

The colonists were now free to form a new nation. It would be a nation ruled by laws, not kings.

In late May of 1787, representatives from each state arrived in Philadelphia. These representatives would plan the new government. They would write the Constitution.

▲ Delegates from the colonies met at the State House in Philadelphia for what was called the Constitutional Convention.

The delegates spent the summer talking about the new government. They fought about what type of government they should have.

They wrote and rewrote the Constitution many times. Finally, on September 17, 1787, they approved the final document.

The delegates agreed that the states had to ratify, or approve, the new Constitution. Each state called a special meeting. State leaders found a problem. The document did not have a list of citizens' rights.

Today, we consider the United States' ▶ Constitution one of the most important documents ever written. Yet, at the time of its creation, many argued that it was a deeply flawed document because it did not contain a list of the citizens' rights.

Personal Perspectives

"It astonishes me to find this system approaching so near perfection as it does . . . I consent . . . to this Constitution because I expect no better and because I am not sure that it is not the best."

—Benjamin Franklin, Constitutional delegate
   from Pennsylvania, 1787

The Bill of Rights

Many people thought that rights, such as free speech and freedom of religion, were very important.

Fortunately, leaders had the power to change the Constitution and correct mistakes. This was the **amendment** (uh-MEND-ment) process. The power to change, or amend, the Constitution means that as times change, the Constitution can also change.

The people wanted a bill of rights. On June 8, 1789, James Madison wrote ten amendments to the Constitution. He presented them to the new Congress. After much debate, Congress and the states passed the ten amendments. These first ten amendments are the **Bill of Rights** (BIL UV RITES). They became law in 1791.

They Made a
Difference

James Madison

James Madison was a young delegate from Virginia when he arrived at the Constitutional Convention in Philadelphia. Well-educated, he became the major author of the Constitution and has been called the "Father of the Constitution." Later, as a member of Congress, Madison wrote the Bill of Rights. He became the fourth president of the U.S. from 1809–1817.

▲ James Madison

◀ Bill of Rights

21

The First Amendment

Most people believe that the First Amendment is the most important part of the Bill of Rights. It guarantees five civil liberties, or freedoms. They are:

1 Freedom of Religion

The government cannot show preference for one religion over another. It must keep religion and government separate. This concept is called the separation of church and state.

2 Freedom of Speech

Freedom of speech includes what people say and what they write. It includes other forms of expression as well. For example, what you wear or what bumper stickers you put on your car are part of your freedom of speech.

3 Freedom of the Press

The government cannot shut down publications or punish members of the press who criticize the government.

4 Right to Petition

This freedom allows citizens to make a formal request to the government, such as to right a wrong.

5 Right to Assemble

The government must allow citizens to gather in groups for peaceful purposes, such as to create change.

Cesar Chavez put his First Amendment ▶ rights into action.

Limits to the First Amendment

The First Amendment guarantees some important rights. Sometimes groups do not agree about how those rights should be used.

The majority—the largest group—makes the laws. But, the rights of the minority—the smaller groups—must be protected.

The First Amendment

	CIVIL RIGHT	LIMITS
FREEDOM OF RELIGION		
1	You have the right to worship as you wish. No town or state can decide that only certain groups can worship.	A town can say no to the majority display of religious symbols or prayers if they take away the rights of minority religions.
FREEDOM OF SPEECH		
2	You have the right to express your opinions in spoken or written words. No town or state can decide that only some people have free speech.	A town can say no to hate speech or speech that endangers public safety. The federal government can limit tobacco advertising.
FREEDOM OF THE PRESS		
3	The press has the right to investigate, criticize, and print. No town or state can decide that only certain people or groups can publish.	The press cannot print made-up stories about someone (that's called libel). There are times when cameras aren't allowed in a courtroom and when privacy has to be respected in gathering the news.
RIGHT TO PETITION		
4	Citizens have the right to make a formal request to the government, such as to protest an unfair law or wrongdoing.	Congress and the Supreme Court have limited this right by ignoring petitions on certain issues, such as slavery and sedition.
RIGHT TO ASSEMBLE		
5	People have the right to peaceably assemble, or come together. They may assemble in protest or in support of an issue as long as the gathering is nonviolent.	No town or state can decide that only certain groups can assemble. But a town can require a permit that says when and where the assembly takes place.

Checkpoint
Talk It Over

Limits on citizens' rights have been put in place to protect all citizens. Do you agree with the limits placed on citizens' rights? Talk it over with a partner.

The Second Amendment

The Second Amendment gives citizens the right to bear arms. The words *to bear arms* means "to carry a gun." People argue about this amendment. Today, some people think citizens should not own guns. Other people disagree.

The Third Amendment

The Third Amendment says that citizens do not have to let soldiers live in their homes. This right comes from when the colonists had to let British soldiers live with them. This is not an issue today.

The Fourth Amendment

The Fourth Amendment says that no one can search a citizen's house, car, or things without good reason. Legal papers saying that the police have a good reason to search must be granted by a judge.

▲ In our democracy, no one can search your home without a good reason. This protects your home and your right to privacy.

The Fifth, Sixth, Seventh, and Eighth Amendments

The Fifth, Sixth, Seventh, and Eighth Amendments promise fair trials. These amendments protect citizens accused of a crime who have a court trial.

The Fifth Amendment says that all legal matters have to be done fairly. In other words, it provides **due process** (DOO PRAH-ses) of law. The Fifth Amendment also says that the government cannot force a citizen to be a witness, or give evidence, against himself or herself. And it says that if a citizen is put on trial and found not guilty, that person may not be put on trial again for the same crime. Being put on trial for the same crime twice is called **double jeopardy** (DUH-bul JEH-per-dee).

The Sixth Amendment is the right to a lawyer and a fair and speedy trial. It also promises that the trial will be judged by a jury of one's peers, or fellow citizens. The Seventh Amendment is the right to a trial by jury in civil court. The Eighth Amendment is freedom from cruel and unusual punishment.

The Ninth and Tenth Amendments

The last two amendments limit government power.

The Ninth Amendment says that even if a right is not in the Bill of Rights, it does not mean that citizens do not have that right.

The Tenth Amendment gives powers not given to the federal government either to the states or to the people.

▲ Most juries are made up of twelve jurors, and usually the verdict, or decision, must be unanimous.

The Thirteenth, Fourteenth, and Fifteenth Amendments

The men who wrote the Constitution had to make many compromises. They could not agree about slavery. Some states wanted slavery. Other states did not. The Constitution did not outlaw slavery.

As time passed, the disagreement about slavery led to the Civil War. The North and South fought from 1861 to 1865. After many deaths, the North won the war.

George Washington was one of many early leaders who owned slaves. Here, a slave is holding Washington's horse. ▶

In 1870, the Fifteenth Amendment was passed, giving male African Americans aged twenty-one and older the right to vote.

Abolitionists (a-buh-LIH-shun-ists) were people who were against slavery. During the Civil War, abolitionists worked to amend the Constitution.

The Thirteenth Amendment became law in 1865. This amendment ended slavery. After the war, the Fourteenth Amendment was passed in 1868. It gave citizenship to former slaves.

Then, in 1870, the Fifteenth Amendment was passed. It said that the rights of citizens to vote were not to be denied because of race or color. This amendment gave male African Americans the right to vote.

▲ African Americans were able to vote for the first time after the Fifteenth Amendment was passed.

SUMMING UP

- On July 4, 1776, America declared independence from Great Britain. The Declaration of Independence contained the idea that "all men are created equal."

- Colonial leaders wrote the Constitution and later added the Bill of Rights.

- The Bill of Rights gave individual rights to citizens, such as freedom of speech, religion, and trial by jury.

- After the Civil War, the Thirteenth, Fourteenth, and Fifteenth Amendments granted rights to African Americans.

Putting It All Together

Choose one of the activities below. Work independently, in pairs, or in groups. Share your answer and what you have learned with the class.

1. Reread pages 22–26 on the Bill of Rights. List the rights in what you think is the order of greatest to least importance. Then explain why you listed them in that order.

2. Twenty-seven amendments have been added to the Constitution since 1787. Why do you think it is important that amendments can be added to this document?

3. Look at the painting on pages 16–17. Then find a photo of today's Congress online or in the library. Compare and contrast these images. What is similar about these representatives? What is different?

FACTORY WORKER'S DILEMMA
CARTOONIST'S NOTEBOOK • ILLUSTRATED BY MICHAEL BORKOWSKI

SMITH & CO. MACHINE SHOP, NEW YORK, NY, 1910

WE HAVE TO WORK THE NIGHT SHIFT AGAIN WITHOUT PAY.

AGAIN? THAT'S EVERY NIGHT THIS WEEK.

WILL THAT BE A PROBLEM?

NOT AT ALL, SIR.

NO, SIR!

IF I HEAR ANYONE IN THIS FACTORY HAS JOINED A UNION, YOU'RE OUTTA HERE— CITIZEN OR NOT! THERE'S PLENTY OF MUTTS LIKE YOU GETTING OFF THE BOAT EVERY DAY . . . NOW GET BACK TO WORK!

I CANNOT SIGN THAT! I WILL LOSE MY JOB! I HAVE A FAMILY TO FEED!

PSSSS! WE MUST STAND TOGETHER! SIGN THIS PETITION!

SHHH! WE DON'T WANT ANY TROUBLE, WE JUST BECAME CITIZENS.

WHAT SHOULD HE DO?

- SHOULD HE SIGN THE PETITION AND JOIN THE UNION?
- WHAT DO YOU THINK WILL HAPPEN IF HE DOES?
- WHAT DO YOU THINK WILL HAPPEN IF HE DOESN'T?

Chapter 3

PROTECTING Citizens' Rights

How does the U.S. government protect citizens' rights as times change?

After the Civil War, Congress gave African Americans equal rights. But over time, some states took these rights away. Who had the final say: the federal government or the states?

The leaders who wrote the Constitution built in a way to fix that problem. They gave the Supreme Court the power to interpret, or decide, what the Constitution means. This is called **judicial review** (joo-DIH-shul rih-VYOO).

Brown v. Board of Education

African Americans did not have equal rights in the South. African Americans could not go to school with whites. They could not sit or eat in the same places. This is called segregation (seh-grih-GAY-shun).

Essential Vocabulary
judicial review page 32

▲ This is Linda Brown in her segregated classroom.

African Americans began to demand equal rights in the 1950s. They wanted fair laws.

In 1896, the Supreme Court said segregation was legal. They said that states could have "separate but equal" places for black people and white people. But public places for African Americans were not equal.

African Americans began to demand equal rights in the 1950s. They wanted fair laws. So they turned to the courts. One case in 1952 was very important. This case was *Brown v. Board of Education of Topeka*.

Linda Brown was an eight-year-old girl. Brown lived in Topeka, Kansas. She was also African American. She had to walk many blocks to an all-black school. But the white school was much closer. The Browns wanted Linda to attend the nearby white school. The school district refused.

▲ Thurgood Marshall (center) and two other NAACP lawyers celebrate their victory in the *Brown v. Board of Education* school desegregation case.

Thurgood Marshall

The National Association for the Advancement of Colored People (NAACP) took the case. Thurgood Marshall led the team of NAACP lawyers. He said that black children did not get the same education as white children. He said that "separate" could never be "equal." He convinced the Supreme Court. In 1954 the justices said segregation was unconstitutional (un-kahn-stih-TOO-shuh-nul). It was against the law.

Checkpoint

Read More About It ✔

Research more about Linda Brown and what happened to her as a result of the court's decision.

Everyone thought that segregated schools would be outlawed right away. Instead, most states in the South did not make changes. Using the courts was not always enough.

People protested. The government passed new civil rights laws. This period became known as the civil rights movement.

▼ Brave citizens, like this woman in the sunglasses, stood up against adversity.

▲ African Americans protested segregation and, in time, won their civil rights.

Miranda v. Arizona

"Anything you say can and will be used against you in a court of law."

You have probably heard these words on TV. They are part of the Miranda warning. Police have to say these words to any person they arrest.

The events that led up to the case of *Miranda v. Arizona* began in early 1963. The police in Phoenix, Arizona, arrested Ernesto Miranda for a series of crimes.

Miranda was a young, uneducated man. He did not know his rights. He did not know that a citizen has the right to remain silent. He did not know that a citizen cannot be forced to be a witness against himself. He also did not know that he had the right to a lawyer.

The police took advantage of the situation. They lied to him. The police said witnesses had already named him.

▲ Ernesto Miranda (at right) was later convicted of the crime he confessed to, but the decision in his landmark case still protects all people accused of crimes.

Primary Sources

Miranda Warning

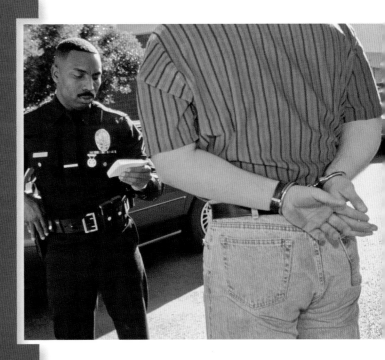

1. You have the right to remain silent.

2. Anything you say can and will be used against you in a court of law.

3. You have the right to talk to a lawyer and have him or her present with you while you are being questioned.

4. If you cannot afford to hire a lawyer, one will be appointed to represent you before any questioning if you wish.

5. You can decide at any time to exercise these rights and not answer any questions or make any statements.

WAIVER

Do you understand each of these rights I have explained to you? Having these rights in mind, do you wish to talk to us now?

The Supreme Court Hears the Case

The police spent hours asking Miranda questions. Finally, the young man confessed to the crimes. At his trial in June 1963, Miranda was convicted and sentenced to a long prison term.

Two lawyers took on the case. They asked the Supreme Court to review the case. Miranda's lawyers argued that the police had ignored Miranda's civil rights. They had not followed the Fifth and Sixth Amendments. But the lawyers for the state of Arizona disagreed. They said forcing the police to read suspects these rights would do more harm than good.

Because ideas and customs change over time, the Court's interpretation of the Constitution has changed, too.

In June of 1966, the justices decided in favor of Miranda. Winning the case did not help Miranda. He was still found guilty and sentenced to prison. However, Miranda did help protect others accused of crimes.

Interpreting the Constitution

In these cases, a citizen's rights were violated. It is the job of the Supreme Court to think about the meaning of the Constitution and apply it to each case.

The Supreme Court has the power to interpret, or understand the meaning of, the Constitution.

Ideas and customs change over time. For this reason, the Court's understanding of the Constitution has changed, too. These changes can affect citizens' rights. They can also protect citizens' rights from government abuses of power.

These were the nine Supreme Court justices in 2010.

Samuel A. Alito Jr.   Ruth Bader Ginsburg   Stephen G. Breyer   Sonia Sotomayor   Clarence Thomas

Anthony M. Kennedy   John G. Roberts Jr.   Antonin Scalia   Elena Kagan

SUMMING UP

- The Constitution gives the Supreme Court the power of judicial review, which is the power to interpret the Constitution.

- Because ideas and customs change over time, the Court's interpretation of the Constitution has changed sometimes, too.

- These changes can affect and, in some cases, are made to protect citizens' rights.

▲ Supreme Court of the United States

Putting It All Together

Choose one of the activities below. Work independently, in pairs, or in groups. Share your answer and what you have learned with the class.

1. You are a lawyer. You have to plead your case before the Supreme Court. Reread pages 32–38. Choose a case. Tell what rights you are fighting for, and use constitutional amendments to support your view.

2. You are a reporter. You have to interview Linda Brown. Write five questions you would like to ask her. Role-play the interview with a partner.

3. The Supreme Court justices serve for life. Why is it important for the justices to be fair when they interpret the Constitution? Explain your answer.

Living as a
U.S. Citizen

Remember Ezell Blair Jr. sitting at the lunch counter in Greensboro, North Carolina? That Monday, February 1, 1960, was just the beginning of a great struggle for equal rights.

On Tuesday of that week, twenty-eight students arrived and sat down at the counter. On Wednesday, students filled almost every seat at the counter. On Thursday, three white students joined the group of African American students. And by Friday, hundreds of students sat down at lunch counters around the town.

Greensboro was in the national news. Town leaders tried to end the sit-ins. On April 21, more than forty students were arrested. The African American community held a boycott. They refused to buy from local businesses. The businesses suffered. At last a settlement was reached.

The Smithsonian Institution in Washington, D.C. has a section of the Greensboro lunch counter on display. ▶

CONCLUSION

On July 25, 1960, the first African American ate a meal at the counter of a local store. The African American community had won!

This change proved all citizens have rights. It also proved that citizens can change laws for the better.

1773

Colonists protested for their rights at the Boston Tea Party.

1865

The Thirteenth Amendment ended slavery.

The Constitution was ratified in 1787. The Bill of Rights was added.

The Fifteenth Amendment gave African American men the right to vote.

1791

1870

Citizens can change laws for the better . . . the power rests with the people.

1920

The Nineteenth Amendment gave women the right to vote.

1960s

Citizens like Cesar Chavez fought for the rights of laborers.

Brown v. Board of Ed. outlawed segregation in schools.

U.S. citizens elected the first African American president in the country's history.

1954

2008

How to Write an Editorial

The First Amendment grants American citizens the right to express themselves freely. We can speak out in support of an issue. We can also use writing to raise our voices up against something. One way to do this is to write an editorial. An editorial expresses an opinion in response to events or issues in the news. An editorial can inform, support, criticize, praise, or entertain. Citizens' rights are often the topic of editorials. Write an editorial about a topic or issue that affects your rights. Here are the steps to write an editorial.

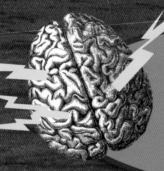

Brainstorm

- Pick an issue that is important to you.
- Prewrite.
- List your ideas and thoughts on the issue.

Write

- Choose your best reasons. Put each reason and the ideas that support it in a separate paragraph.
- Hints: Editorials should be brief and direct. Provide facts to back up opinions. Be clear and use a positive tone.

Revise, Edit, and Proofread

- Check your editorial to be sure you have stated your opinion and your reasons clearly.
- Check your spelling, grammar, and punctuation.

Sample Editorial

Where's My Book?

Imagine going to your local public library to find a favorite book and discovering that it had been banned, or removed from the library shelves! Why? Because a local group demanded that the book be banned. Some of the most famous and popular books in the world have been banned.

Book-banning is really about censorship, or removing ideas that someone thinks are harmful. Groups sometimes object to a certain book because those people don't approve of the book's content. But public libraries serve the entire community, not special interest groups. People should have freedom of choice in what they read. Banning books takes away our freedom of choice.

We live in a democratic society. That means we should have the constitutionally guaranteed right to choose what we want to read. The First Amendment protects our right to know. So we should not ban books.

Glossary

abolitionist (a-buh-LIH-shun-ist) *noun* a person who worked to outlaw slavery (page 28)

alien (AY-lee-en) *noun* a person who lives in the United States but is not a citizen (page 14)

amendment (uh-MEND-ment) *noun* a change to the Constitution (page 21)

Bill of Rights (BIL UV RITES) *noun* the first ten amendments to the Constitution (page 21)

citizen (SIH-tih-zen) *noun* a person who was born in the United States, born outside the United States to U.S. parents, or who applied for and was granted citizenship (page 6)

civil rights (SIH-vul RITES) *noun* the individual rights that all members of a society have to freedom and equal treatment under the law (page 10)

Constitution	(kahn-stih-TOO-shun) *noun* the written plan for the government of the United States (page 9)
democracy	(dih-MAH-kruh-see) *noun* a form of government in which power rests with the people (page 6)
double jeopardy	(DUH-bul JEH-per-dee) *noun* being put on trial for the same offense twice (page 26)
due process	(DOO PRAH-ses) *noun* the idea that laws must be fair (page 26)
immigrant	(IH-muh-grunt) *noun* a person who leaves one country to live permanently in another (page 14)
judicial review	(joo-DIH-shul rih-VYOO) *noun* the power of the Supreme Court to interpret the Constitution (page 32)
naturalization	(na-chuh-ruh-lih-ZAY-shun) *noun* the process of becoming a citizen (page 11)
permanent resident	(PER-muh-nent REH-zih-dent) *noun* a person who is living in the United States but is not yet a citizen (page 14)

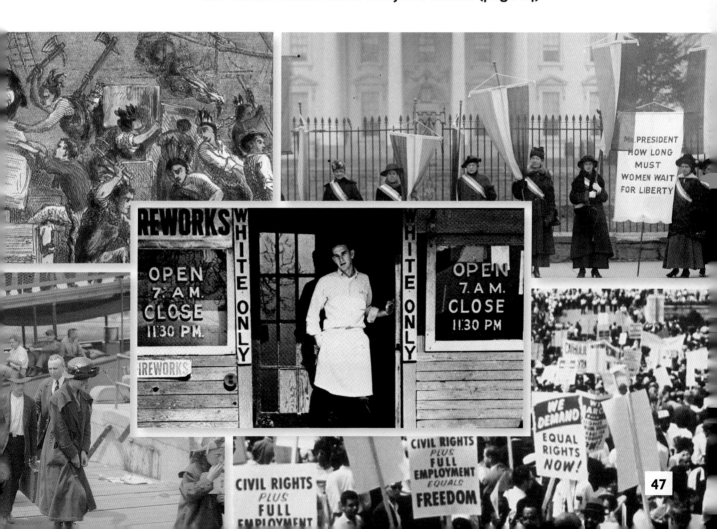

Index